First Lady Chronicles

Life as a Pastor's Wife

First Lady Chronicles – Life As A Pastor's Wife

Copyright © 2019 by Kyna Kemp

All rights reserved. Published and Printed in the United States of America. No part of this book may be reproduced or transmitted in any form or by any means without written permission from the author.

Published by: Kyna Kemp

Email: ktkempauthor@gmail.com

Cover design and book formatting by Aneitra S. Scott
Details 'R Essential
www.detailsressential.com

ISBN: 978-0-9993431-1-1

Dedication

To all Pastors' wives, past, present and future. You are loved and appreciated.

Dear Pastor's Wife,

For consistently supporting your husband spiritually, emotionally, and physically...thank you. Your love is his greatest earthly treasure.

For filling in the 'gaps' at church, for noticing the little things...thank you. It makes a difference.

For smiling when your own heart is breaking...thank you. That takes grace.

For all of your sacrifices, both visible and invisible...thank you. God sees them all.

For being authentic, for not trying to be superwoman...thank you. People can always relate to real.

For modeling Godly living and for mentoring those who are young in the Lord...thank you. The next generation is changed because of this.

For bearing up under criticism and attack; for responding with humility, grace, and forgiveness time after time...thank you. You are like Christ in your suffering.

For navigating an often hectic and unpredictable schedule with graceful flexibility...thank you. You make it look easy.

For burying your own grief; for setting your own burdens aside, in order to reach out and minister to others in their times of sorrow...thank you. People will never forget that you were there for them.

For nurturing your relationship with Christ above any other relationship...thank you. It shouldn't be any other way.

For leading through an example of servanthood, for serving with confidence and joy...thank you. You compel others to serve God with you.

For embracing the privilege and high calling of ministry, for saying "yes" to life with a pastor...thank you. You make Christ's bride look beautiful.

XOXO,

A Kindred Spirit
(March 31, 2015)
https://hopeforpastorswives.com/2015/03/dear-pastors-wife-thank-you/

First Lady Chronicles

Life as a Pastor's Wife

Presented by: Kyna Kemp

Introduction

Traditionally in the church, the First Lady is also referred to as the Pastor's wife. Although the duties of the Pastor's wife are not defined, typically her role is to encourage and support her husband in the ministry; cover him in prayer, and ensure he has everything he needs to lead the congregation. Additional duties include taking care of the family and being active in the church. Under the perceived glitz and glamour, there is a woman who is often hurt, ignored, stressed, neglected and overwhelmed. In order to meet all the expectations, the life of a Pastor's wife can be a blessing as well as a struggle.

As a preacher's kid, I have a been surrounded by Pastors' wives all my life and have seen first-hand how their faith and trust in God has allowed them to persevere on this journey. The First Lady Chronicles is a compilation of life-changing experiences from pastors' wives which provides insight into what it is like to walk in their shoes. This book is written for pastors' wives to know you are not alone and to provide resources to help you through this journey. When difficult situations arise, know that God is always with you and will provide everything you need to fulfill your calling. I pray this book encourages and inspires you to be the First Lady God has equipped you to be. Embrace the call; you are Built for this!!!

Table of Contents

Dedication — i

Introduction — v

Chapter One — 1
Prayer-Our Power Source
Glenda Ancrum-Adams, Author

Chapter Two — 13
Role of a First Lady (What it Means to Me)
Pastor's Wife Before and After
Dorothy Herron, Author

Chapter Three — 27
Pastor's Wife
THIS IS NOT WHAT I ASKED FOR!
Sonia Starks, Author

The Pastor's Wife — 39
Poem

About the Visionary — 41

Chapter One

Prayer – Our Power Source

Glenda L. Ancrum-Adams, Author

I heard a testimony by Lady Gwendolyn Washington, the second wife of Bishop F.D. Washington, many years ago and she talked about how if you really want power with God you need to establish a prayer life. Lady Washington began to expound on the power of prayer. At the time, she indicated that she prayed every morning at 5:00 a.m. That testimony inspired me to establish my own personal prayer time at 5:00 a.m. every morning, and it has been my weapon against the enemy through every situation in my life.

What is Prayer? The most basic definition of Prayer is "talking to God." Prayer is the opportunity God gives each believer to become intimately acquainted with him. Although, prayer is the most powerful spiritual weapon a believer can possess, it is the weapon we use the least. Almost all our prayers begin with rushing to God with our problems, our needs, and our irritations (we don't cherish that time with God). Then there are some of us who pray what I'd like to call "soap opera" prayers…here's how we sound, "now God, I know I haven't been much of a church person, but I really need your help, and if you help me, I promise I'll turn my life around." Sound familiar? It's too bad prayer is often viewed as a last resort…something to use only in emergencies, when it only takes a few moments of your time.

Prayer was not uncommon in the Old Testament…a good example is Hannah, who was barren…she had not bore children because the Lord had shut-up her womb. Peninnah, the other woman in her household, ridiculed, teased, provoked and considered Hannah to be worthless because she was childless. But we won't find Hannah popping her neck, snapping her fingers, putting her weave in a ponytail, pulling off her earrings, or putting on her sneakers ready to fight Peninnah. No, scripture says she prayed. Hannah went to the Lord in prayer, and the Lord began to fill all the cracks of her so-called damaged life, he filled the cracks of her broken spirit and out of what was considered damaged goods, God brought a miracle named Samuel.

Prayer was not uncommon in the New Testament, like many of our churches today, their church was built on Prayer:

- Acts 1:14 – the churched was birthed by ten days of passionate prayer.
- Acts 3:1 – Peter and John were going to church for the purpose of prayer.
- Acts 4:31 – they prayed for boldness to preach, and they were filled with the Holy Ghost
- Acts 6:4 – the apostles focus on the power of prayer and the Word
- Acts 9:40 – Peter prayed and raised Dorcus from the dead
- Acts 10:9 – Prayer opened the doors for the Gospel to be preached to the Gentiles

Now, there were a lot of things missing from the new testament church. They lacked character, committees, strategies, and church buildings (things some would consider vital for church health). But they were a church that believed "Men ought always to pray, and not to faint," St. Luke 18:1. Prayer had been their sustaining power amid storms and a weapon that guaranteed results.

Who or What is a First Lady? The leading woman of an art or profession (Merriam-Webster Dictionary). However, in the home, the First Lady is more than a profession, a pretty hat, fine dress, or red-bottom shoes. First Lady is more than a trophy in a display case. The First Lady is a Wife and Mother who is often occupied with dirty dishes and laundry. At times she is also the Doctor, Disciplinarian, Caregiver, Nurse, Career Woman, Counselor, and an ATM Machine ☺. Behind that pretty face, her life is often dictated by the demands of her husband and children.

In the church, you'll find the First Lady has held many positions such as: the New Members' Class Teacher, Prayer Warrior, Prayer & Bible Teacher, Sunday School Teacher, Pianist, Organist, Choir or the Choir Director, Drummer, Announcement Clerk, and Sermonic Soloist. If necessary, the First Lady will also preach the sermon. This multi-talented caring woman is an individual in her own right and certainly one that deserves praise. The First Lady often makes great sacrifice to make sure the needs of God's people are met.

In the beginning God created the heaven and the earth. However, God's creative work was not complete until He made woman. He could have made her from the dust of the ground, as He made man. God chose, however, to make her from the man's flesh and bone. In so doing, He illustrated for us that in marriage man and woman symbolically become one flesh. Genesis 2:24 says, "Therefore shall a man leave his father and his mother and shall cleave unto his wife: and they shall be one flesh." From this scripture we learn that because the First Lady and her husband are one, his concerns are her concerns, his triumphs are her triumphs and his failures are her failures. For they are ONE...she is his encourager, when he is discouraged, she is his cheerleader when the roar from the crowd has ceased. The First Lady is her husband's partner.

Out of all the hats the First Lady wears, she can handle all these job descriptions because of prayer...it is her Power Source. When we speak of a Power Source – we speak of a source of power. In my studies, I've found that there are several types of power:

#1 – **Solar energy** is radiant light and heat from the Sun that is harnessed using a range of ever-evolving technologies such as solar heating, photovoltaics, solar thermal energy, solar architecture, molten salt power plants, and artificial photosynthesis. (Wikipedia)

#2 - **Nuclear power** is the use of nuclear reactions that release nuclear energy to generate heat, which most frequently is then used in steam turbines to produce electricity in a nuclear power plant. As a nuclear technology, nuclear decay, and nuclear fusion reactions. (Wikipedia)

#3 – **Wind power** or wind energy is the use of airflow through wind turbines to provide the mechanical power to turn electric generators and traditionally to do other work, like milling or pumping. (Wikipedia)

But the type of power that is most common to us is Electric Power. Electric Power is the rate at which electrical energy is

Prayer – Our Power Source

transferred by an electric circuit; usually produced by electric generators or batteries. (Wikipedia). As we commune with God in prayer, the power of God is transferred into the spirit man and gives us the energy to endure any trial or test that arises in our lives.

It is important to note the First Lady is a person who hurts and bleeds just like you. She desires, love, attention, and affection, just like you. She likes to know she is important in her husband's life and that she doesn't play second fiddle to anyone else. She is often heartbroken, ignored, and her office is disrespected, yet she continues to wear a smile despite it all. She is not a novice in salvation…she knows that outside of her title, she is simply a sinner saved by grace. She too is one who must work out her own soul salvation with fear and trembling. You don't need to preach to her, for at the end of the day if her soul is not right before God on judgement day, she already knows where she'll spend eternity.

I've found in life that there are many young women whose one mission in life is to be a First Lady. Be careful what you ask for and please proceed with caution. For things are not always as glamorous as they seem.

I became a First Lady on August 15, 2005…my husband and I were not strangers to each other. We were always friends. We were both Preacher's Kids (PK's) and were raised in the

same church circles. After we were married, we were amazed to find out how closely knit our parents were. His dad and my dad served in

Vietnam together, ...and when my family first moved to New York, my parents lived with my husband's family, until they found their home. My husband and I sang together in District and Jurisdictional Choirs. At times, after church we'd meet for dinner and go to our separate homes when dinner was done. One day all of that changed. We became romantically involved; thus, friends became lovers and then marriage.

I never intended to be married to a Pastor, because my Mom's experience as a First Lady was not the most pleasant and I had no intention of going through some of the things that she experienced. However, when you fall in love with someone, you become a part of everything they are a part of.

I was taught by my former Pastor, Superintendent Charles Bond, that regardless of our positions, accomplishments or achievements in church or life, the saving of souls must remain a priority. Superintendent Bond told me that God is only concerned with who has accepted the Lord Jesus Christ as their personal savior (in other words, "God's business is soul business"). Acts 1:8 says, "that we would receive power after we receive the Holy Ghost, and that we would be Christ witnesses...". With that mindset, I am not your average First Lady. I am the type of First Lady, who seeks the least likely to be greeted after church is over...I am the one who actually witnesses to (not walk away from) the Homosexual or Lesbian and tell them, that in spite of where you are right now, Jesus loves them and wants to give them new life...I am the one who takes the beggar to the restaurant, buys the meal and witness to them while they eat it...I am the one who will buy the clothes for the prostitute to wear to church...I am the one who will minister to the alcoholic, in spite of what his breath smells like. For if souls are God's priority, it should be the priority of every believer.

I have had many experiences as a First Lady, both good and bad; in fact there are so many that I wouldn't be able to share in one chapter. However, I have been able to press forward because of my position in prayer.

If you are experiencing adversity, hardship, struggle, or a circumstance in your life, that seems insurmountable; I encourage you to take it to the Lord in prayer. As we communicate with God in prayer, He begins to change the circumstances and situations that surround us. For James 5:16 tells us that "The effectual fervent prayer of a righteous man availeth much." Therefore, we don't have to accept what man says or what our situations look like – God hears your cry, He hears your groan, He sees your tears, and He's coming to your rescue. So, don't throw in the towel, don't give up, don't get weary, don't get discouraged, don't faint, don't surrender, don't retreat, you will win if you don't quit. Romans 8:37 tells us that "Nay, in all these things, we are more than conquerors through Him that loved us." Someone penned a song that says, "Don't stop praying the Lord is nigh, don't stop praying, He'll hear your cry, the Lord has promised, His word is true, don't stop praying He'll answer you.

How often should we pray? St. Luke 18:1 says, "Men ought to always pray and not faint." David tells us in Psalm 55:17, "Evening, and morning, and at noon, will I pray, and cry aloud: and he shall hear my voice."

I believe many of our prayers are hindered because we don't believe God has the power to do what we're asking him for. But Hebrews 11:6 reminds us that "...for he that cometh to God must believe that He is and that He is a rewarder of those that diligently seek Him."

What I like about prayer is that there is no special posture in prayer...some people like to kneel in prayer as did Solomon in 1 Kings 8:54 and Daniel in Daniel 6:10 (for it is a sign of humility). There are some who like to stand and pray as did the Pharisee in St. Luke 18:11...some like to lay prostrate before the Lord as did Jehoshaphat in 2 Chronicles 20:18 and Jesus in the Garden of Gethsemane in Matthew 26:39...sometimes you only have time to pray riding in your car or walking around your house – Lord save, Lord heal, Lord deliver, Lord set free, Lord have mercy, Lord lift the heavy burden, Lord let the oppressed go free. Your posture in prayer doesn't matter to God. For Isaiah 65:24 declares, "And it shall come to pass, that before they call, I will answer; and while they are yet speaking, I will hear."

Not only is prayer our power source, but the First Lady must use that power source to cover her husband. We must pray against: others slandering his name, being enticed by loose women, becoming overwhelmed, ignoring the voice of God, being led by pew pastors, slothfulness, disobedience, and others taking advantage of his humble heart. The First Lady must pray for more strength and that her husband: is led by the spirit of God and not his flesh, remains sensitive to the voice of God, keeps a spirit of prayer on his lips and is the Man of God that God is calling for in these last and evil days.

In St. John Chapter 17, Jesus prepares to move towards His death on the cross that will cover the sins for the entire world. Jesus prays for His own glorification; He prays for His disciples, and then He prays for all believers.

About the Author

Lady Glenda Ancrum-Adams

Lady Glenda Ancrum-Adams was born to anointed parents, who both were immersed in their aspect of ministry: her dad, the preacher and her mother, the anointed singer. God anointed Glenda with the voice of her mother and the preaching of her father.

As a vessel of honor, the Lord favored Lady Adams to travel in cities such as Northport, Alabama, Oakland, California, Boston, Massachusetts and was truly humbled by the opportunities that have been afforded her.

Lady Glenda Adams accepted Christ into her life at an early age. In 1992 Lady Adams received her license as an Evangelist in the Church of God In Christ. In 19997, she served as District Missionary of the Progressive District in the Third Ecclesiastical Jurisdiction of Eastern New York under the leadership of spiritual father Bishop Frank O. White.

From her humble beginnings as the middle sibling out of 4 other siblings, Glenda was blessed to share in ministry with great gospel choirs. Her solo debut launched her into a singing career with these choirs.

As the Lord continues to bless and anoint Lady Glenda-Ancrum, she was asked to sing with some of Gospel greats such as

Prayer – Our Power Source

Pastor Donnie McClurkin, Marurette Brown-Clark and the Curt Karr Singers, Kim Burell, to name few. Lady Glenda also sang in the State Shekinah Choir with Dr. Frank A. White.

    Lady Adams is an active member of her local church, Healing Temple Church of God in Christ under the leadership of her husband, Superintendent Robert A. Adams, where she is involved in many sectors in ministry. Lady Adams has one beautiful daughter, LaShaye D. Paschal-Monroe, and four beautiful grandchildren: Kennadie, Harper, Parker, and Charlotte. Lady Adams strives to be an example of a virtuous woman, a woman who has yielded to God in every area of her life.

    Lady Adams has a heart for the people, she is a steadfast prayer warrior, and she continues to push towards the mark and produce excellence in all her ministry opportunities.

    For booking information, please contact Ms. Danielle Henry @ (954) 993-6337 and/or Mrs. Erika Brown @ (347) 458-9245

Author contact information:
Glenda L. Ancrum-Adams
55 So. 32nd St.
Wyandanch, NY 11798
(516) 642-5501
Vesselofhonorinc22@gmail.com

Chapter Two

Role of a First Lady
(What it Means to Me)
Pastor's Wife Before and After

Dorothy Herron, Author

The journey began in the early part of 1972. I met Travis Dell Herron in February 1972, and we married in November 1972. He was not a

Role of a First Lady (What it Means to Me)
Pastor's Wife Before and After

minister, nor a pastor at the time. In December 1972, he got the call, mind you just one month after our wedding ceremony.

I could really go back to the age of 2 years old when I was stricken with polio. At that age, I had no idea what happening to me, but there were many witnesses in a small country community in Tennessee. The community consisted of large families, the historical Marshall Chapel which includes elementary school and the family church in honor of our grandfather, Johnny Marshall.

I survived polio, due to family members holding vigil around the clock on my behalf. There were no doctors close by, so they depended on healing directly from God. The only side effect was I had to learn to talk and walk again, and I lost all my hair. Normally the opposite occurs especially the walking. When I became of age to understand, I was constantly told I survived due to God having a special call on my life; this was in 1948.

I had no idea what the call meant, nor did I understand who or what the call was to, nor did I care to seek to find out. Mind you I was number 13 out of 17 children, I was the last girl with three younger brothers. I was constantly reminded of this call, so I would often ask why me, why did this call fall on me. Most of the seniors in the community did not have anything but an elementary education, but they were God-fearing people. They couldn't explain in detail the different challenges that we would face nor could they predict too far into the future (oh just me).

Dorothy Herron

Growing up, I was what you called very shy, with not much confidence in myself. But I was what you call (before my time) because I stayed close to the older mothers listening to their council or instructions, and to tell the truth; most were not too welcoming. Especially after I went on to high school, it was from elementary first grade to eighth grade and on to high school, no in-between. In high school which was some miles from my community, and I was bussed to school, and it was there I began to be exposed to different cultures outside my close knitted community. I begin to want to explore other adventures, like going to parties, dating, etc. I did or do believe those seniors mothers had that six sense; they would often say things to make you wonder who was talking to them. It put fear in me to be mindful of my call that I just couldn't do or be what others tried to make me be.

I survived high school, but I wanted to move away and start another journey I wanted to invest in. I did work after school to help my parents; their only income was farming, and it was seasonal. I had two sisters who were married and had adventured West to California. I had studied some of the history and cultures of California, so I wanted to come and do my own things. In July 1969, I moved to California. One of my sister's said I could live with her, but upon arriving, I needed to look for work because she didn't say that she would support me. So, I decided to go to college. I attended MTI Business College, taking a full course in Computer.

Role of a First Lady (What it Means to Me)
Pastor's Wife Before and After

My desire for the world was growing, so I began adventuring out after meeting a few friends. Mind you, my sisters were in church and deeply involved, so that meant I couldn't go crazy. I ended up moving in with my other sister who had a husband and six children. She was more involved in her church than the other sister, but I liked the atmosphere. But I still thought I would have the freedom to go and come as I please, for some reason I didn't fit in, how crazy is that. I would go to church with her and sit with the kids in the back of the church. I would drive her around the city (she could not drive) to doctor appointments for the kids, take her shopping, etc.

By her involvements in the church, I began to meet other young people, and I became involved with church activities, local, district and state, as they say the rest is history. I have never regretted the day I said yes to God, mind you, I had not started looking for my calling. But I found myself still being drawn to the older mothers in the church who took me under their wings (or should I say under their protection).

In 1972 as I stated earlier, I met Travis, who was saved from a street life of drugs, gangs, etc. Totally different from what I was accustomed to, I had no idea. When the Lord saved him, he wanted to go back and tell all his friends and acquaintances about his experience with Jesus, which was a strong calling from God. Many could not believe he had made a transformation from being a street thug to telling them about Jesus. Through him, many came to know the Lord, many became devoted members of our church, and some went on to become Ministers, Pastors, Missionaries and strong lay members to the body of Christ.

As time would have it, he was called to preach, became involved in the total ministry of the church, jail, and street ministry. So that immediately put me in the middle of it all, and this involvement led him to start his own church. The first location was in the area, *The Fillmore*, where he got saved. We started out with some members who were not familiar with the church but just wanted to be saved. The name of our first church was "Jehovah," and that is when I became a Pastor's Wife.

The area we were in was not welcoming, non-believers were beginning to buy up the housing units. One couple lived above the church and often complained of the noise coming from our church, so, the landlord would not sign our lease agreement when it was up. The price of building and the cost associated with starting a new church became too expensive, so we folded and went to an already established church, where we were former members. We just went back home with a few added members.

This is where I could understand the call that was on my life from the beginning of my infant life. In San Mateo, the Pastor's wife became my mentor, First Lady Jemmie Swindell, who was the sister of Mother Helen Macklin in Palo Alto. First Lady Swindell has continued to be my mentor. When Evangelist Herron would often be asked to come to New Sweet Home Church of God in Christ to run revivals, I would often go with him. I was welcomed and embraced

Role of a First Lady (What it Means to Me)
Pastor's Wife Before and After

with so much wealth and knowledge of how the First Ladies supported their husbands. I will forever cherish and continue to reach back to the memories of how they set the pace for me being a young woman.

In 1995, we got a call from a church in Pittsburg, CA, where the Pastor/Superintendent John Moore & First Lady Juanita Moore were pastoring at the time. Pastor Moore was also an Evangelist, and he traveled all over the country, he often traveled to our National Meeting along with First Lady Moore, but this particular year he asked Elder Herron to come and run a revival while they were gone to the National Convocation. After returning he had the heart attack, he could no longer function as a full-time Pastor, the First Lady and the congregation asked our Jurisdictional Bishop W. W. Hamilton to find a replacement.

Bishop Hamilton came and appointed Elder Herron as the Elder-in-charge at the demise of Pastor Moore in 2000. In 2001, Elder Herron was appointed the Senior Pastor at the Greater McGlothen Memorial Temple COGIC, the beginning of my biggest challenges. If I tell you each setting was different, it was. In this situation, I was more accepted than he was, and to me that was a very bad place to be in. You had to sit through the pros and cons of the challenging members; it seems each challenge became I thought "unbearable." But because of Elder Herron's street life, he developed a no fear of people, and he stood the test of times. It took some weeding out of those who gave the most trouble, mostly by moving their memberships to other churches, but God. I must give credit where credit is due the support of Mother Moore helped me stand the test of times because she remained supportive and faithful to our Ministry along with the former family adult children and the grandchildren.

In 2013, due to illness and a lot of health issues, Pastor Herron started looking for a replacement, he said to the Elder who he asked to come and work with us his intention would be to turn the church over to him and his wife. Pastor Herron voiced his decision to our now Bishop J.W. Macklin. In 2018, the Elder Coleman Starks was appointed as new Senior Pastor at the Greater McGlothen Memorial Temple COGIC, Elder Herron bid him God speed and that he takes the church to the next level.

I've enjoyed the ride, through the good, the bad and the ugly from each experience and I have learned to take everything to God in Prayer, as he won't tell anybody else. You cannot tell your members even your most trusted the business of the church, remember your friend has a friend, and they have a friend, and the list goes on and on, only tell Jesus. Nineteen years as a First Lady has taught me compassion, a stronger love for people, the history is too long to list, somethings I will just ponder them in my heart and spirit.

My suggestions to any Lady that has taken the role (not by her choosing) of a Pastor's Wife, is to do as the scripture says in Proverbs 3:5-6 KJV

Role of a First Lady (What it Means to Me)
Pastor's Wife Before and After

> *V. 5 Trust in the Lord with all thine heart; and lean not until thine own understanding.*
>
> *V. 6 In all thy ways acknowledge him, and he shall direct thy path.*

Remember First Lady; we have come into a dual role, first a wife, and mother (if there are children, especially if they are small). I remember in the olden days, where we were not allowed to do ministry outside of the home if there were small children present. During the old days, mothers would come to your house and teach you how to cook, clean and how to take care of your children. I totally value those teachings and doing by examples.

Many of my duties at our church were to open, clean up, that means to open the service and all until the preaching of the Word. As time progressed it took a lot of my shyness away, and I learned to delegate some of the responsibilities on to others, and the Lord blessed.

My husband taught me to have compassion and look out for the welfare of the members. I had to learn who could take constructive criticism and who could not so easily, and that means they are to be treated no differently. Trust me; God will give you wisdom, patience, and love for the people of God because we are family in the family of God.

Trust me there were days when I wanted just to take a leave of absent, but God kept reminding me of my calling and that He, Jesus and the Holy Spirit had not given up on me.

I want to end with this quote by Lorna Dobson who is the First Lady of Calvary Church in Grand Rapids, Michigan, where her husband serves as Senior Pastor, and I quote:

"We have our own set of expectations about our Role as Wives of Ministers. We have another perceived set of what we think the congregation has of us, a set from our husbands, and one from the Board (as well as) …. What our mentors said to us in preparation for life in the ministry, or what was not said.

- You will or can destroy yourself, trying to please everyone.
- Have fun being a Minister's wife, enjoy being whom God made you.
- Don't have a key to anything whether you are part on a pedestal or trampled under the foot, Pastor's Wives everywhere will be able to relate to the adventures and advice of other more experienced and committed women of your rank.

Be encouraged, you are not walking this journey alone, especially when managing your Christian commitment to serve and your personal commitment to the congregation and their families."

Be Blessed!

Former First Lady Dorothy Herron

Emeritus.

Role of a First Lady (What it Means to Me)
Pastor's Wife Before and After

There are three highly recommended books that I have read and taken the strongest points from.

1. ***I'm More Than a Pastor's Wife, by Lorna Dobson***
2. ***When is a First Lady ever First, by First Lady Barbara J. Warren McKinney?***
3. ***Heart to Heart with Pastors' Wives, by Lynne Dugan***

About the Author

Lady Dorothy Louise Marshall Herron

Born to the late Elmer George & Mae Francis Marshall in the City of Medon, Tennessee. She is the 10th of 17 siblings with five remaining. Dorothy is the youngest girl of her siblings; therefore she had to learn to survive among three younger brothers and one brother a year older than her. Dorothy was stricken with polio at the age of 2 years old. Her Pastor & Uncle held a vigil around the clock asking God not only to spare her life, but to heal her also. God answered their prayers with a charge on her life.

Dorothy grew up as a Country Girl, went to Marshall Chapel Elementary School, named after her Grandfather. She attended West High School in Denmark Tenness as number 7 of 230 students with an "A" plus grade average. Upon graduation, she went to work for Jackson Madison County Hospital in Central Supply. Dorothy worked there until she moved to Jackson, Mississippi to stay with her second oldest sister who was confined to bed because of a pregnancy that was threating her and her baby's life. After the baby was born, she continued to live in Jackson, Mississippi and got a job working for Presto Manufactory.

One of Dorothy's dreams was to live in California. In July 1969, Dorothy moved to Daly City, California, to live with another

Role of a First Lady (What it Means to Me)
Pastor's Wife Before and After

sister, Sadie and her family. In 1970, she enrolled at MTI Business College located downtown, San Francisco, where she completed a full semester in Computer Technology. She worked several small jobs in and around San Francisco.

In 1980, she was later employed by General Electric and became the Data Processor Supervisor. In 1990, General Electric moved the company to Los Angeles, by that time she had met and married Travis, so she remained in San Francisco. The Lord blessed her to be employed by the City and County of San Francisco Water Pollution Control. Dorothy worked her way up the ranks and became Executive Secretary to the Manager for 15 years in that one location. She went as high as her position would allow. In 1995, she went back to work in the private industry, where she was employed by Business Development Inc., which became a joint venture with four other Consulting Businesses. The major project accredited to them is the new San Francisco International Airport.

In 1969, after arriving in California, she visited her sister's, Ruby Jenkins church, True Hope COGIC. It was during a revival conducted by Evangelist Larry Moore; he prophesied that the Lord had a call on her life; that day, she recommitted her life to the Lord. At that time, she was the only single young lady in the church, but the Lord kept her busy until he blessed others to get saved, namely, Travis Herron.

In 1972, they were united in holy matrimony at the Faith Temple COGIC. The Lord blessed this union with two son, Torrance

D'Mon and Thyeus Dell, three daughters Lori, Trini and Jackie, today they are blessed to have nine grandchildren, and one great-grand. Dorothy served as the First Lady and member of Greater McGlothen Memorial Temple, COGIC for over 20 years. She served as District Missionary to the Morning Star District, she was installed by the late Mother Mattie McGlothen in 1986. Dorothy was also appointed as Jurisdictional Marshall and the Jurisdictional Secretary for the Women's Department, Program Chair, California Northwest Women's Convention. She also served with Dr. Mary Welch in same positions and was appointed as an Executive Board Member, her last assignment; she was appointed Assistant Treasurer and Registration for the Jurisdiction and the National.

Dorothy rejoined the workforce in 2005 and worked for an Emergency Family Shelter as a full-time Counselor, for the Shelter Inc. in Martinez, California.

Dorothy is retired and enjoying her journey taking care of her husband, who is a disabled veteran. She is currently a member of Bethel Ministries, where her Pastor and First Lady are Pastor William Hunt and Mother Gloria Hunt, Supervisor of Women for the NorCal Jurisdiction under the leadership of Bishop J. W. Macklin and First Lady Vanessa Macklin.

Dorothy is forever grateful to the Lord for His many blessings. She often says in Lamentations 3:22 – 23, "It is of the Lord's mercies that we are not consumed. Because his compassion fails not. His mercy is renewed every morning great is thy faithfulness."

Role of a First Lady (What it Means to Me)
Pastor's Wife Before and After

She continues to inspire and encourage everyone that she comes in contact with. To God, be the glory for the things He has done.

Chapter Three

Pastor's Wife

THIS IS NOT WHAT I ASKED FOR!

Sonia Starks, Author

Dear New Pastor's Wife:

I'd like to share some things with you regarding your new job, position, and assignment. I'll start with this quote I found the other day. It is in the style of a Want Ad, and it seems to describe our "job" very well.

HELP WANTED: PASTOR'S WIFE

- **Must:** sing, play music, lead youth groups, raise seraphic (angelic) children, entertain church notables, minister to other wives, have ability recite Bible backward and choreograph Christmas pageant.
- **Must:** keep pastor satisfied, peaceful and out of trouble.
- **Must:** be able to deal with difficult colleagues, demanding customers, erratic hours.

PAY: $0.00

You may ask the question, "why would a woman want to be a Pastor's wife?" The answers may surprise you. Yes, there are some women that would love to have this position. Their reasons vary from the gifts given on Pastor & Wife Appreciation Day to basking in the accolades given to the Pastor when he does something they agree with or being seated in the front of any huge service (District or Jurisdictional), with everyone watching. However, a lot of us do not focus on those things. Most of us, we see this position, as the most challenging and yet sometimes rewarding assignment, we've ever had. Sometimes, the hours are long, and at times, a balancing act between children, your job (if you work inside/outside the home), household chores, "taking care of your husband" (whatever that may entail), and finally the church family (congregation). As a matter of fact, if there are pastor's wives like me, they can honestly say, **"This Is Not What I Asked For!"**

My experience as a Pastor's wife started later in life, actually at the age of 64 years old. I know some would say, that's starting late in this position, but God obviously has a plan. I am a Preacher's kid (PK), the oldest of four children. My two sisters have been in their "positions" as Pastor's wives for years. However, for me, it started in February 2018, when my husband was installed as a Pastor. In February 2019, we celebrated our 1st Pastor and Wife Anniversary. But let me start at the beginning……

Our beginning:

In February 1974, I said, "I do," to Mr. Starks. One month later, he left for the Air Force, and in August of the same year, we joined him in Texas where he was stationed. Growing up as a preacher's kid, my prayer was always, "I don't want to be a preacher/pastor wife and will not marry one."

<u>Well, God honored the first part of the statement.</u> When we got married, my husband wasn't saved. He was a member of another denomination, and while there is nothing wrong with that, he wasn't committed to that faith. Meaning, he hardly attended church (unless his mother made him), didn't pay tithes or offering, and complained about how much money his mother was giving to the preacher. So in my mind, I thought "this is cool since he didn't have a problem with me going to church, I can work with this situation. Thank you, God!" Well, that was short-lived…..

What happened next:

A year before my husband was honorably discharged from the Airforce, we hitched a ride with another soldier looking for a church in Sacramento, and we came across Gospel Center COGIC. It was there, during a revival, the Lord saved my husband, sanctified and filled him with the Holy Ghost, and when he got up from the altar, he said God had called him to the ministry, well I lost it and began to cry. The people were saying, "look at Sister Starks, she's so happy, but that was not why I was crying, I was crying because I was telling God, "that's not what I asked for." Little did I know, that when we entered the church that Sunday, it would be the beginning of our spiritual journey for over 20years. The bible confirms this in Isaiah 55:8, which reads, "My thoughts are nothing like your thoughts, says the Lord. And my ways are far beyond anything you could imagine."(NLT).

It was a learning process for both of us. For example, while he was learning how to preach (expound on the Word, when to make an altar call, etc.). I was learning how to be a preacher's wife. Such as getting used to sitting in the front, dressing appropriately, searching for my role in the church and most importantly praying for him. As a preacher's wife, sometimes you may feel invisible, and I did. Taking nothing away from my husband, because he is God's man but sometimes the people (unintentionally most times) will make you feel invisible. For example, before my husband became a pastor, he held various positions in our local church, as well as our jurisdiction such as: Chairman of the Trustee Board, District Sunday School Superintendent, then promoted to Jurisdictional State Sunday School Superintendent, as well as Jurisdictional State Auxiliaries In Ministry

(AIM) Chairman, interacting with Pastors, their Sunday School staff, superintendents, auxiliary leaders and their churches as a whole.

While I loved how they respected and appreciated his working with them, sometimes I didn't feel like part of the team. For example, he had a wonderful group of people working with him in different areas of California. This particular night, we drove to one of the churches to surprise one of his Sunday School Area Workers. They were putting on a Sunday School program/service. We arrived safely and entered the church. As we entered the sanctuary, they immediately recognized my husband, and ushered him straight to the front, leaving me behind. At that moment, I wasn't sure if I should follow him up front, or take one of the vacant seats in the back. So I stood there until he was seated. He looked back and noticed I was still standing at the door. He beckoned for me, and then one of the "escorts" brought me up front. Now, growing up in church I understand, the respect the people have for the Man of God, but they forget sometimes he is not alone. So, do not take it personally.

My first example of a Pastor's wife is my mom. She stood by my dad's side for over 20 years. When you're a pastor's kid, your home life and church life seems blended together. Not only did she work in the home, but she also worked as dad's assistant. That's why there was a time when I considered her the Assistant Pastor. My dad had two churches and while he was at one church in Roosevelt, NY, mom would go out to the other one in Westbury, NY. Mom would preach, sing, pray, make an altar call, oversee the offering and come home with a report to dad regarding the service. When they were in service together, she was always reserved but available if dad needed her to do something in the service, which usually meant singing before he preached. When we were growing up, mom lead most of the songs and my siblings, and I was the choir. However, as time went on and our church membership grew, we were no longer the only choir members.

When it came to disagreements between my mom and dad, the congregation never saw that side. She never rolled her eyes or "cut-up" during service even when she disagreed, not even in the car on the way home from church. Even at home, we never knew what their disagreements were about, because back in those days, "their discussions" were always behind the closed doors of their bedroom, and if we were around, we were usually sent outside to play or to our room.

If you will allow me to be transparent, I didn't learn <u>that</u> lesson too well. Now, I didn't "cut-up" in church, and I even smiled when I didn't appreciate what he was saying, but alone in the car with him was different. For example, one time we were arguing in the car all the way to the church. We pulled into the parking lot, and some of the saints were getting out their cars. As I got out the car, one of the saints said, "Hey Sister Starks," and I returned the greeting and talked for a few minutes. As the sister walked inside the church, I turned to close the car door, and he said, "you're a hypocrite, you were just mad at me, and now you're smiling and talking to them."

I smiled and said, "I'm not a hypocrite, they didn't do anything to me, but until we get it straightened out, I'm still mad at you." I smiled and walked in church. (pray for me)

Another area for a pastor's wife to be aware of is his health. As a pastor's wife, you want the people to keep respect for your husband. Not making him seem perfect, but showing them that in spite of his personal challenges, he is still capable of being the "Watchman over their soul." But when he is struggling with health issues, I believe you try harder, to not let the people see much, if any of that side. You both need their prayers, not their pity. As we get older, sickness is a fact of life, but it is not always looked at understandably when you're a pastor. Sometimes, I think Pastors are looked at, like people used to look at the "mailman." There is an unofficial motto of the post office that says, "Neither snow nor rain nor heat nor gloom of night stays these couriers from the swift completion of their appointed rounds." Or like the energizer bunny commercial, to "keep going, and going and going." Meaning regardless of what the situation or their health, they are expected to go to every service, answer all their calls (whether day or night), and just be available. However, with the help of the Lord, the pastor can keep moving with prayer and a time to rest.

<u>Being a Pastor's wife can be scary</u>. I believe there will always be (at least in the beginning) questions like: How do I act? Where do I sit? How do I dress? However, like Eve, we're the "help meet," so then the questions become, when do we give him help? How much

help do we give? How do you proceed, when God gives you an idea for the church? When do we back off, and let God do it?

<u>Being a pastor's wife is more than a notion.</u> You smile when you want to cry or yell, and you keep stuff bottled up inside because you're taught that you can't be confidential with people your husband pastors. Most importantly, you **"cover"** him; like when he makes a scriptural mistake during his message or when he tells the congregation <u>only</u> about your behavior in a situation that took place between the both of you, or when he's struggling with health issues.

When I talk about "covering your husband/pastor," I'm reminded of a scene in the movie called the Preacher's wife (with Whitney Houston and Courtney Vance). In this scene, Whitney Houston's husband is fumbling with his message and the congregation is getting restless, and some are going to sleep, so she gives him what I call the "Pentecostal boost," to help get his message over to the people. A pentecostal boost is when the wife (usually) gives the preacher/pastor a boost during his sermon, by yelling the word "Yes" or "Go ahead preach," with a melody.

Some women become pastor's wives when they marry a pastor, others become a pastor's wife, when their husband, who is the Assistant Pastor, takes over the leadership role of Pastor upon the Pastor's death. Then there are those who become pastor's wives, when God calls their husband to start a church. However you get the position, you need to ask God, "what can I do?" So you begin to think: I can take on additional chores at home so that he can focus on the ministry. I can pray with him and for him (remember, he's only human). I could allow him "downtime," let him be alone when needed, or sit quietly next to him until he's ready to talk. Other things you may do: make notes and discuss later or on the way home (if it's just you and him) in the car make suggestions. Don't feel bad if the suggestions are not always accepted. I think sometimes; they don't realize or remember we're in the pew also, so you see and hear what everyone in the congregation sees and hears, only difference is you love him enough to tell him. So for this job, I believe you need the following things (I know there's more).

1. <u>You must be saved</u> - You must have a relationship with Christ because you will need to keep in touch with Him on a regular basis! For the pastor and for yourself.
2. <u>Don't be jealous</u> - Be watchful and observant. Song of Soloman 8:6 says, "Set me as a seal upon your heart, As a seal upon your arm; For love is as strong as death, Jealousy as cruel as the grave; Its flames are flames of fire, A most vehement flame."
1. <u>Don't be insecure</u> - This is not a competition. Work on your own ministry. Even though you are his "help meet," God has gifted you to do in work in the kingdom also, so work on it. If you don't know what it is, ask the Lord! Proverbs 18:16 says, "A man's gift makes room for him, And brings him before great men."
2. <u>Remember your vows</u>. "For better, for worse, for richer, for poorer, in sickness and in health, to love and to cherish, till death do us part." Keep communication open; pick a time to

talk. It won't always be easy but can be done with the help of the Lord.

3. <u>Find another Pastor's Wife to confide in</u>. If you're not sure who, ask the Lord, He knows the right person. Why confide in a pastor's wife? Because you have a lot in common….you're in the same working-class and work it is. If you are the pastor's wife, someone is looking to confide in; **confidentiality is the key.**
4. <u>He belongs to God and the Church</u>. Remember, he may be your husband, but he belongs to God and the church. You and the children are on the list of priorities, just not first.

If your husband is a pastor Jeremiah 3:15 tells us how God looks at them, "15 And I will give you pastors according to mine heart, which shall feed you with knowledge and understanding."

Finally, I found this prayer by Sarah E. Frazer, and I pray it ministers to you, as it did to me: "**Dear Lord, as I come to pray for my pastor's wife, let me name her: ____. You see her not in her role, but who she is in you: daughter, beloved, forgiven, and enough. Satisfy the longings of her heart and keep her eyes focused on you. I pray your word speaks to her today.**"

About the Author

Lady Sonia Starks

Sister Sonia Starks is a resident of Sacramento, California. She has been married to Elder Coleman Starks for 45 years. They have four children and six grandchildren. She is a retired California Department of Transportation (Caltrans) Equal Employment Opportunity (EEO) Trainer.

Sister Starks accepted Christ at age 15. She grew up, the oldest of four in the church as a "PK" *(Preacher's Kid),* under the leadership of her parents Pastor David and Missionary Blanche Ancrum at Saint's Memorial Church of God in Christ, Roosevelt, L.I., New York.

She currently serves as a member of Greater McGlothen Memorial Temple Church of God in Christ, Pittsburg, California, under the leadership of her husband, Pastor Coleman Starks. She has served in the following capacities: Sunday School, Prayer & Bible Band, and New Membership Class Teacher, Scholarship Committee President, Asstistant Financial Officer, Choir and Praise Team Member, and Soloist.

She has also served as Sacramento, Stockton, Modesto-Area Vice President of California Northwest Jurisdictional Music Department under the leadership of State Choir President-Eld. Joseph Lockhart.

The Lord has also blessed her with the following Musical Ministry Opportunities:

- The Martin Luther King Celebration Choir
- The Sacramento Component Choir (Gospel Music Workshop of America)
- Featured Soloist-California Northern 1st Jurisdiction Workers Meeting
- Featured Psalmist-Saint's Memorial COGIC (Boston, Massachusetts)

She loves the Lord and gives all the praise to Him for all the wonderful ministry opportunities and prays that the Lord will continue to use her to bless His people.

by Judy Dycus, March 10, 1992

https://www.my-pastor.com/pastors-wife-poems.html

She's a Godly woman, she has such grace
Always a warm greeting, a smile on her face.
She's always encouraging, she knows her place.
She is - The Pastor's Wife.
She has to always look just right
Always on time, though the schedule's tight.
From early morning, 'til late at night
Always - The Pastor's Wife
She's such a Lady, everyone's friend
She serves with love from deep within.
All the rifts she tries to mend
Oh she's - The Pastor's Wife
She carries your burdens; she prays for you
Sometimes she cries the whole night through.
But you won't know when she's feeling blue,
Cause she's - The Pastor's Wife
At church as she starts to walk up the aisle,
So many need to stop and talk for a while.
Though she is tired, she has her own trials

She's patient, she's - The Pastor's Wife
Her life, her time, is not her own
There's always a need, they go on and on
With a knock at the door, or a ringing phone.
That's the life of - The Pastor's Wife
Her husband she shares with a whole congregation
She humbly accepts his intense dedication.
In loneliness she kneels to see consolation
God Bless - The Pastor's Wife
She will someday reach the end of this race
As she meets her Master face to face
Surely our God has a Special Place

In Heaven for - The Pastor's Wife!

About the Visionary
Kyna Kemp

Kyna Kemp is the owner of On Point Mobile Notary Services and is a fully bonded and insured Notary Signing Agent. She has been performing general notarizations as well as loan document signings for the past 15 years. She prides herself in offering excellent customer service, attention to detail and same day service. She services the Sacramento, Elk Grove, Folsom, Roseville and surrounding areas and will travel for customer convenience.

Kyna Kemp has worked for the State of California for over 18 years. Her education, experience and hard work have helped advance her career over the years. She currently works as a Manager, which allows her to coach, empower, and train staff. Kyna is also an Empowerment Coach who specializes in the areas of career advancement, personal development, organization and time management. She empowers individuals to reach their goals and identify the fears and obstacles keeping them being successful.

Kyna Kemp became an author in October 2016 when sharing her story in the book compilation Stand Up Be Heard, Part II. Her book, Birthing Kings was released in August 2017. She is currently on her next book **_The First Ladies Chronicles,_** which will be released at the end of 2019.

Kyna Kemp can be reached at (916) 572-7332 or via email at KTKempAuthor@gmail.com.

www.ingramcontent.com/pod-product-compliance
Lightning Source LLC
Chambersburg PA
CBHW030916170426
43193CB00009BA/881